BBC

DOCTOR WHO

FOUR DOCTORS

"Sparkily captivating dialogue smartly turns the promise of a team-up into a dramatic pleasure. A beguiling story, well worth your time."
TOO BUSY THINKING ABOUT COMICS

"If you don't know squat about *Doctor Who,* everything you need to know is held in the pages of this singular, sensational book."
THE BUY PILE

"Brilliant writing from Paul Cornell, excellent artwork from Neil Edwards and an amazing color palette from Ivan Nunes make this a perfect comic!"
FLICKERING MYTH

"A fun ride that packs a punch!"
FANSIDED

"Brilliant internal dialogue and subtle interactions!"
DAVID TENNANT NEWS

"Something special!"
NEED TO CONSUME

"I never expected anything as awesome as this! A must-have."
SNAP POW

"An airtight, continuity-packed time-traveling crossover epic delivered at breakneck pace!"
INFINITE COMIX

"This was great! A+"
SCIFI PULSE

"Delivers the most interesting insight so far into what makes the Doctor tick."
BIG COMIC PAGE

"Fun, thrilling and surprising in equal measures, sure to be just what any fan wants from a Doctor Who event."
NERDS UNCHAINED

"Not only a good media tie-in comic, it's a good comic, period!"
COMIC BOOK RESOURCES

"Worth the cover price for the staggering artwork and the intriguing storyline!"
STARBURST

TITAN COMICS

EDITOR
Andrew James

ASSISTANT EDITOR
Kirsten Murray

COLLECTION DESIGNER
Rob Farmer

SENIOR EDITOR
Steve White

TITAN COMICS EDITORIAL
Lizzie Kaye, Tom Williams

PRODUCTION SUPERVISORS
Jackie Flook, Maria Pearson

PRODUCTION MANAGER
Obi Onuora

STUDIO MANAGER
Selina Juneja

SENIOR SALES MANAGER
Steve Tothill

SENIOR MARKETING & PRESS OFFICER
Owen Johnson

COMICS BRAND MANAGER
Lucy Ripper

DIRECT SALES & MARKETING MANAGER
Ricky Claydon

COMMERCIAL MANAGER
Michelle Fairlamb

PUBLISHING MANAGER
Darryl Tothill

PUBLISHING DIRECTOR
Chris Teather

OPERATIONS DIRECTOR
Leigh Baulch

EXECUTIVE DIRECTOR
Vivian Cheung

PUBLISHER
Nick Landau

Special thanks to Steven Moffat, Brian Minchin, Matt Nicholls, James Dudley, Edward Russell, Derek Ritchie, Scott Handcock, Kirsty Mullan, Kate Bush, Julia Nocciolino, Ed Casey, Marcus Wilson and Richard Cookson for their invaluable assistance.

BBC WORLDWIDE

DIRECTOR OF EDITORIAL GOVERNANCE
Nicolas Brett

DIRECTOR OF CONSUMER PRODUCTS AND PUBLISHING
Andrew Moultrie

HEAD OF UK PUBLISHING
Chris Kerwin

PUBLISHER
Mandy Thwaites

PUBLISHING CO-ORDINATOR
Eva Abramik

DOCTOR WHO: FOUR DOCTORS

HB ISBN: 9781782765967
SB ISBN: 9781785851063
Published by Titan Comics, a division of
Titan Publishing Group, Ltd. 144 Southwark Street,
London, SE1 0UP.

A CIP catalogue record for this title is available from
the British Library. First edition: January 2016

10 9 8 7 6 5 4 3 2 1

Printed in China. TC0868

Titan Comics does not read or accept unsolicited
DOCTOR WHO submissions of ideas, stories or artwork.

BBC

DOCTOR WHO

FOUR DOCTORS

WRITER: PAUL CORNELL

ARTIST: NEIL EDWARDS

COLORIST: IVAN NUNES

LETTERS: RICHARD STARKINGS AND
COMICRAFT'S JIMMY BETANCOURT

TITAN
COMICS

BBC

www.titan-comics.com

DOCTOR WHO

FOUR DOCTORS

GABBY
GONZALEZ

Gabriella Gonzalez is a young would-be artist from Sunset Park, Brooklyn, New York, who is traveling the universe at the Tenth Doctor's side. Her youthful spirit and artistic eye are coupled to an adventurous and quick-witted mind.

TENTH
DOCTOR

The Doctor is an alien who walks like a man. His Tenth incarnation is trying to get over his post-Time War guilt by sprinting along in a happy-go-lucky guise – but he keeps shooting himself in the foot, because all his guilt, rage and frustration is buried just underneath.

ELEVENTH
DOCTOR

The Doctor is the last of the Time Lords of Gallifrey. His Eleventh incarnation is a gangly boy professor with an old, old soul. Not guilty or embarrassed about anything, he has made mistakes some enormous! – but owns each and every one.

PREVIOUSLY...

The Doctor is an immortal time traveler who, when mortally-wounded, regenerates into an entirely new body.

He has worn many faces in his long and adventurous life.

When the fabric of the universe is threatened, when the laws of time, space and all of reality start to break down...

...on those dire days, different incarnations of the Doctor can meet.

It should never happen. But this is one of those days...

TWELFTH DOCTOR

The Doctor is never cruel or cowardly, he champions the oppressed across time and space. His Twelfth incarnation is done with guilt, wants to fix things, and now he feels he has licence to – and doesn't have to be a happy, fun Manic Pixie Dream Doctor to do so.

ALICE OBIEFUNE

Former Library Assistant lice Obiefune has grown into a courageous hero since her avels with the Eleventh Doctor egan. Having put the death of ° mother behind her, Alice now braces all that traveling in the TARDIS can offer her.

CLARA OSWALD

Clara Oswald has known the Doctor through both his Eleventh and Twelfth incarnations, and has stuck with him through thick and thin, witnessing all manner of strange, wonderful and terrifying things. A teacher at Coal Hill School, she juggles her 'real life' with her secret adventures in the TARDIS!

BBC

DOCTOR WHO

FOUR DOCTORS

WRITER
PAUL CORNELL

ARTIST
NEIL EDWARDS

COLORIST
IVAN NUNES

LETTERER
RICHARD STARKINGS AND COMICRAFT'S
JIMMY BETANCOURT

GABBY'S SKETCHBOOK ARTIST
ARIANNA FLOREAN

EDITOR
ANDREW JAMES

ASSISTANT EDITOR
KIRSTEN MURRAY

DESIGNER
ROB FARMER

"THAT'S IT, LADS. THEY'VE HIT THE *CHRONIC TRIPWIRE*.

"THE DALEKS IN THERE ARE EXPERIENCING SOMETHING THEY'LL FIND MOST UNPLEASANT --

"-- ACCELERATED EVOLUTION.

"SEND IN YOUR WAR BANDS IF YOU LIKE, BUT LET ME ASSURE YOU --"

-- I HAVE TO
KE THIS RIGHT.

ELEPATHIC CIRCUITS,
DO YOUR STUFF.

ERE'S WHERE
NEED TO BE."

PARIS, 1923.

THANKS.
YOU KNOW
WOULDN'T DO THAT
UNLESS IT WAS
IMPORTANT.

FOR THE
SAKE OF EVERYTHING...
I HAVE TO PREVENT
THIS.

ACROSS TOWN.

-- AND THEY ACTUALLY THOUGHT --?

-- IT WAS A BRILLIANT IDEA TO RAID THE FRENCH GOLD RESERVES! I *KNOW!*

IT'S LIKE VAMPIRES WANTING ALL THE GARLIC.

YEAH, AND IN THIS CITY, GABBY, THAT'S THE VERY NEXT THING WE MIGHT HAVE TO --

-- OOH, CREPES. I HAVEN'T HAD A CREPE SINCE THAT CONFIDENCE-BUILDING LUNCH WITH JOAN OF ARC --

-- WHICH WENT A BIT *TOO* WELL --

SHALL WE CREEP IN, HAVE A CREPE AND CREEP OUT AGAIN?

I WAS *HOPING* WE'D GET TO EAT.

WELL THEN --

-- NOT ALLONS-Y, THE OPPOSITE, STAYUNE PUTTIQUE!

THAT'S THE THING ABOUT SPEAKING ALL THE LANGUAGES, YOU DON'T GET TO LEARN THEM.

YOU ORDER ALL THE CREPES --

"-- I'LL DISPOSE OF CYBES HERE IN A RESPONSIBLE MANNER."

OW! OW OW OW!

YOU COULD HAVE USED THE OVEN GLOVE. I'M JUST SAYING.

ALICE OBIEFUNE! I'M NOT GOING TO SAVE THE WORLD FROM RADIATION MONSTERS COMING OUT OF THE SEINE USING A TATTY OLD OVEN GLOVE!

IF IT HAD BEEN A *COOL* OVEN GLOVE, THAT WOULD HAVE BEEN *PERFECT.*

AND I DIDN'T GET TO SAY ANYTHING CLEVER ABOUT THEIR CHOICE OF RIVER, BECAUSE THEY WEREN'T INSANE *AT ALL.*

IT'S ALL A BIT OF A LET-DOWN. BUT AT LEAST NOW I CAN GO AND BUY FRENCH COMICS.

WAIT A MO --

-- THESE STREETS SEEM VERY FAMILIAR, AND I REMEMBER THAT CAFÉ IS GREAT, FOR SOME REASON.

DO YOU REMEMBER WHO DODGED THOSE RAYS TO *FETCH* THE OVEN GLOVE?

WHY DON'T YOU GET A COFFEE --

WHILE I AND FIND E LOVELY ANDES SSINÉE?"

GABBY GONZALEZ, ALICE OBIEFUNE, YOU DON'T KNOW EACH OTHER, AND YOU DON'T KNOW *ME* --

-- BUT WE ALL KNOW THE *DOCTOR*. OR A *DOCTOR*.

AND NOW I'VE GOT FIVE MINUTES TO *CONVINCE* YOU OF SOMETHING, OR THE UNIVERSE WILL BE DESTROYED.

MIND IF I SIT DOWN?

SORRY IF I DON'T ACCEPT THAT STORY *IMMEDIATELY*. WHAT'S THE BOX CALLED?

THE TARDIS.

WHAT DOES HE USE TO --?

SONIC SCREWDRIVER. FOR EVERYTHING.

SHE'S TELLING THE TRUTH. JUST *LISTEN* TO HER! *BOTH* OF YOU!

SHE SAYS *THAT*, YOU DON'T GET ALL "WHAT'S HER PROBLEM?", YOU GET INTO IT, START TAKING IT APART.

WE'RE *DOCTOR* PEOPLE, LADIES.

OKAY. SO. PLEASE GET THAT I DON'T WANT US TO COMPARE NOTES MORE THAN NECESSARY. IT COULD GET A BIT --

-- TIMEY --

-- WIMEY?

RIGHT. LOOK AT THIS.

OH --!

SO YOU WENT AND TOLD HIM, RIGHT?

IF *THEY* SAW THAT PHOTO, WHAT WOULD *YOUR* DOCTORS BE ABSOLUTELY, COMPLETELY, INCAPABLE OF DOING?

NOT GOING THERE.

RIGHT AWAY.

EVENTUALLY, AFTER HE'D SPENT AGES TRYING NOT TO.

EXACTLY

-- SO DAMN *RIGHT* I DIDN'T TELL HIM. YOUR DOCTORS *WILL* MEET. I WAS *THERE*. GABBY'S DIDN'T *RECOGNIZE* YOURS, ALICE. *NEITHER* COULD HAVE IMAGINED MY DOCTOR *EXISTING*.

THAT'S HOW I KNOW THIS PICTURE SHOULDN'T HAPPEN.

WHEN WE LEAVE HERE, WE HAVE TO MAKE SURE *NONE* OF THEM SET FOOT ON THIS PLANET CALLED 'MARINUS'.

GOT IT? THESE DOCTORS MUST NEVER --

GABBY!

ALI

-- MEET.

OH MY DAYS.

OH NO. OH NO NO NO.

SO *HE'S* THE *NEXT* ME --

-- THE *LAST* ME --

-- ALL RIGHT. I GET *THAT*. FINE.

BUT WHO ARE *YOU*, THEN?

THIS MAN *CAN'T* EXIST, *SHOULDN'T* EXIST!

NOW... WE DON'T KNOW WHAT'S GOING ON HERE.

WHO'S THIS 'WE'?

THAT'S WHAT *WE* NEED TO FIND OUT.

STOP IT!

STEP *AWAY* FROM THE 'MULTI-DOCTOR... EVENT!'

THIS IS *EXACTLY* WHAT I DIDN'T WANT.

I *KNOW* THIS MEETING DIDN'T HAPPEN. THAT EVEN THOUGH TIME CAN BE REWRITTEN --

-- THIS IS A FIXED POINT IN TIME.

ONE POINT TO THE GIRL FROM GRYFFINDOR.

OH, BALONEY --!

OW OW OW!

AH, NOW, THAT WAS THE *BLINOVITCH LIMITATION EFFECT* AT WORK.

WHICH [ME]ANS HE *IS* [TH]E FUTURE [M]E.

RIGHT. WELL DONE. AND HELLO AGAIN, YOU.

I MEAN, *JUST* HELLO. HELLO FOR THE *FIRST TIME.*

BUT WHICH ALSO MEANS...

OKAY, WHEN YOU LOOK LIKE THAT, IT'S TIME TO --

-- *RUN.* USUALLY. FOR MINE TOO.

YEAH. I *BURN* THROUGH TRAINERS.

RIGHT. [Y]EAH. WE [JU]ST CREATED [THI]RTY GREAT [P]ARADOX --

-- AT A FIXED POINT IN TIME --

-- WHICH MEANS --

GOSH, I'M LOOKING FORWARD TO MY REGULAR COMICS ORDER!

NEWSAGENTS ON EVERY CORNER. COMICS AS AN ART FORM. THE CIVILIZING INFLUENCE OF THE FRENCH.

ALTHOUGH, DEPENDING ON THE ERA, THAT CAN ALL SOMETIMES BE *MANDATORY.*

MY BEST CUSTOMER! THANK GOODNESS YOU'RE BACK.

WHEN YOU LEFT A FEW MINUTES AGO --

CCUPATIONAL HAZARD. IF ANOTHER ME HAS NABBED MY COMICS AGAIN--!

-- YOU FORGOT YOUR STANDING ORDER. I FOUND IT UNDER THE COUNTER.

AH! COOL!

THREE MONTHS OF *LE PETIT VINGTIEME!*

FULL OF EVER-SO-SLIGHTLY *RACIST* ADVENTURES, BUT THAT GOT *MUCH* BETTER, WE HAD A WORD.

DO YOU HAVE CHANGE FOR PIRATE TREASURE?

UNLESS THE CAFÉ HAS A PARTICULARLY EXCELLENT *PLAT DU JOUR* --

-- READING THESE IN THE TARDIS LOFT WILL *DEFINITELY* BEAT THE RADIATION MONSTERS AND THE OVEN GLOVE --

-- AS TODAY'S MOST EXCITING THING!

TIME!

COMPANION Cover by Elena Casagrande,
Eleonora Carlini & Claudia SG Iannicello

SUBSCRIPTION Cover by
AJ & Rob Farmer

When the Doctor first told me about his 'other selves', I imagined they'd be...

...like they were from a parallel Universe, or just, like, younger or older.

When he talked about them meeting, I thought, hey, BFFs.

I mean, you meet YOU, you're going to be UNDERSTANDING, right?

You're going to treat yourself with kindness.

Another cup, old me?

Why thank you, original universe me.

-- MAKE A *DECISION*, SOMEONE?!

HE SAID FIND THE OLDEST THING. THIS IS GENUINE --

-- SO OKAY, THAT'S SOMETHING!

DOCTORS, WHAT *ARE* THESE THINGS?!

REAPERS. THEY--

-- IF THERE'S A PARADOX OR TIMEY WOBBLE SOMEWHERE VULNERABLE, LIKE THIS FIXED POINT --

-- THEY SWOOP IN TO *FEED*, TO CLEANSE THE WOUND.

I *THINK* I GOT--

-- DOCTOR, I MEAN *MY* DOCTOR --!

-- LOOK OUT!

WHAT?! THEY'RE CHANGING THEIR SIZE. NOT FAIR!

GERROFF! WHY ARE THEY PICKING ON *ME*?! I'M NOT OLDEST OR YOUNGEST, I'M IN THE MIDDLE!

SO. YES. RIGHT. WHEN IN DOUBT--

--RUN!

IS IT SOMETHING TO DO WITH THE REAPERS? DO THEY CUT OFF ALL THE EXITS?

AH! YES! NOW I REMEMBER YOU! THE ARTY ONE! I LIKED YOU. I REALLY SHOULD HAVE *KEPT* YOU.

YOU SHOULD HAVE... *WHAT*?!

GABBY, THIS IS *EXACTLY* WHAT WE EXPECTED. AND DON'T LISTEN TO HIM.

BOW TIE ME WILL BE HERE IN A SEC, AND THEN--

-- WE CAN TRY TO USE THE SAME ENERGY THAT SUMMONED THE REAPERS --

-- TO POWER AN ESCAPE ROUTE! EXCELLENT PLAN! I ALREADY THOUGHT OF IT!

SO, FIND A SUITABLE TARGET FOR FINGER POKING.

IF WE WAIT UNTIL--!

POKE AWAY! I AM *DEMANDING* THAT YOU POKE ME!

FOR GOODNESS' SAKE--!

-- YOU'RE NOT STILL AT IT, ARE YOU?!

THIS LOT BEHIND ME--

"-- THEY MOVE QUITE FAST!"

SWONNK

YES, THE OLD GIRL WILL FEEL THE ENERGY RELEASE AND PROBABLY DECIDE TO HELP US --

"DECIDE?"

-- BUT ONLY IF WE SEND A CONTAINED, NARROW FOCUS BEAM--

YES, OBVIOUSLY--!

-- NOW, JUST DO WHAT I SAY --

DOCTORS, WHATEVER IT IS --

-- DO IT NOW!

-- WE'RE STILL GETTING *CHASED* HERE!

GOOD. YOU SEE, THIS IS THE PLAN --

AND THE *NEXT STAGE* OF THIS PLAN WOULD BE?

-- GET THEM ALL IN HERE, SAVE THE GOOD CITIZENS OF PARIS!

GLAD TO SEE YOU'RE BOTH KEEPING UP.

BIT MORE RUNNING DOWN CORRIDORS!

GLAD YOU STILL DO THAT!

TO BE HONEST, I WOULDN'T MISS IT.

SKREEEE!

NOW, WE WAIT!

-- THOSE ARE *NOT* YOUR CONTROLS!

THERE'S *HUNDREDS* OF THEM!

YES, THERE'S NO WAY TO TELL JUST HOW MANY ARE IN HERE. I'M ALTERING THE *AIR* TO MAKE IT *OLDER.* MIGHT GET A BIT STUFFY.

DOCTORS, ARE YOU ALL ON THE SAME PAGE?!

YOU'RE PUTTING GABBY AND THE OTHERS IN DANGER...

FOR THE GREATER GOOD!

DO IT NOW!

I SAID WE *WAIT.*

UNTIL WHAT?! UNTIL YOU'VE PROVED YOUR POINT?!

UNTIL *NOW!*

BUT, MOVING SWIFTLY ON, AND SINCE THIS SITUATION IS NOW *WELL* MESSED UP, YOU MIGHT AS WELL SEE THIS --

-- THE IMAGE I TOLD YOU ABOUT --

-- YOU THREE ON THE SURFACE OF 'MARINUS'.

WHEREVER THAT *IS*.

NO IDEA.

ME NEITHER.

OH... WAIT WAIT *WAIT*...

WHY IS IT JUST *US* THREE THERE?

WHAT'S *DIFFERENT* ABOUT US?

...

GENTLEMEN, *WE'RE* DOCTORS FROM *AFTER* THE TIME WAR.

WHATEVER THIS *IS*, IS IT SOMETHING TO DO WITH *THAT*?

AND NEITHER OF US *REMEMBERS* THIS MEETING. WHICH ALSO FEELS VERY TIME WARRY.

SO. WHAT CAN WE DO?

THE REAPERS *WEREN'T* A TRAP. THEY WERE JUST WHAT WAS ALWAYS GONNA HAPPEN IF WE MET UP HERE.

THEY WERE JUST THE WEATHER.

BUT THAT PICTURE... *THAT* IS A TRAP.

AND WHAT DO WE SAY TO TRAPS?

I... GUESS I'LL SEE YOU LATER, GUYS!

I HOPE.

"WHAT DO WE SAY TO TRAPS?"

HOW ABOUT, "SORRY MR. TRAP, BUT WHEN YOU RING MY DOORBELL, I'M HIDING BEHIND THE SOFA"?!

EVEN KNOWING *ALL* THIS, IS HE *REALLY* STILL DOING--

"-- EXACTLY WHAT I WAS *WORRIED* HE'D END UP DOING?!"

SETTING THE COORDINATES FROM THAT IMAGE...

YOU'RE NOT LETTING THOSE TWO *GET* TO YOU, ARE YOU?

WHY ARE WE, YOU KNOW, LEAPING STRAIGHT IN?

OH, GABBY GABBY *GABSTER!*

WE *COULD* CHECK OUT THAT MUSEUM SHE TOLD US ABOUT. BUT I GET THE FEELING WE WOULDN'T LEARN ANYTHING NEW.

EITHER WE SPRING THE TRAP OR WE LIVE IN FEAR.

I DON'T *DO* LIVING IN FEAR.

THE BAD STUFF IS *ALWAYS* GONNA HAPPEN --

-- ONE IS *ALWAYS* GOING TO GET ONE'S HEART BROKEN.

I THINK HE MIGHT ACTUALLY BE *SEEKING* PUNISHMENT.

AND HERE THE REST OF US ARE, FOLLOWING *HIM!*

OKAY, IF WE'RE GOING TO AN ALIEN PLANET, I NEED TO CHANGE CLOTHES.

I THINK I *MIGHT* ACTUALLY WIN A 'LEAST SILLY DOCTOR' CONTEST.

WEIRDLY... YEAH.

VVOORRRP
VVOORRRP

NO SIGNS OF LIFE. DOES IT *SEEM* FAMILIAR TO YOU?

WORRYINGLY. BUT I DON'T KNOW WHY.

YOU'RE PUTTING THE UNIVERSE IN DANGER JUST BY --

AH, NO, ACTUALLY, I'M NOT.

YOU'RE A TEACHER, AREN'T YOU? MARKER ON YOUR FINGERS. I LIKE A TEACHER.

STOP BEING ALL --

STOPPING RIGHT NOW, MISS. THERE IS METHOD TO MY MADNESS.

WHATEVER THIS LANGUAGE IS --

-- AND IT'S WORRYING WE CAN'T READ IT --

-- THE GEOGRAPHICAL COORDINATES ARE PRECISE DOWN TO THE TEENY-TINY. AND YOU SAID THAT MUSEUM TALKED ABOUT SPECIFIC *MOMENTS* --

-- MEANING, IF WE DON'T GET INTO THIS SPECIFIC *POSE*, THE UNIVERSE IS FINE --

-- AND WE CAN SNIFF AROUND A BIT.

CAN YOU KEEP YOUR HANDS OUT OF *ANY* SPECIFIC POSE?

I DON'T KNOW *WHAT* YOU MEAN.

-- FROM *OUTSIDE* OF SPACETIME!

SO WE'RE DEALING WITH SOMETHING FROM BEYOND REALITY?!

DOCTORS--!

AND WE COULD BE TTACKED AGAIN AT ANY MOMENT!

WE NEED TO--

ANALYSE THE BEAM EFFECT!

USE THE TARDIS TO DETECT THE SOURCE!

FIND A MIRROR TO REFLECT--!

DOCTORS--!!!!

YOU'RE NEARLY AT --

NO! *LOOK* AT IT!

MAYBE FIGHTING WITH YOURSELF... *ALWAYS* GETS YOU TO SOMEPLACE LIKE HERE.

THEY *ARE* AT--!

CLICK

GOT IT! IT *HAD* TO HAPPEN --

DOCTOR WHO

'OPEN MIC NIGHT'

BY PAUL CORNELL & RACHAEL SMITH

THANKS, YOU'VE BEEN A GREAT AUDIENCE.

YEAH, BIT *TOO* GREAT IF I'M HONEST. DON'T GET THE APPLAUSE THING VERY OFTEN...

DON'T QUITE *TRUST* IT.

ANYHOO. PLEASE GIVE IT UP FOR...

..."THE COMEDY STYLINGS OF THE NEXT ME", APPARENTLY.

AH. YES. IS THIS ON?

TAP TAP

A FUNNY THING HAPPENED TO ME ON THE WAY HERE...

UT THAT'S ONLY TO BE... EXPECTED, SN'T IT? GIVEN MY LIFESTYLE. AH. THAT'S THE ODD THING ABOUT OBSERVATIONAL COMEDY.

IT ESN'T RK IF RE ALL ERENT.

SO IT SHOULDN'T. BUT IT... DOES.

A BIT... WORRYING.

IF YOU THINK ABOUT IT...

COUGH

THANK YOU AND GOOD NIGHT!

WHAT ARE YOU DOING?!

MAN WALKS INTO A POLICE PHONE BOX.

OW.

· · · · ·

A SET UP, THEN A SURPRISE, REVERSING EXPECTATIONS!

TEXTBOOK STUFF!

COME *ON*, PEOPLE!

COULD WE TRY KARAOKE?

I'VE HEARD IT'S DELICIOUS.

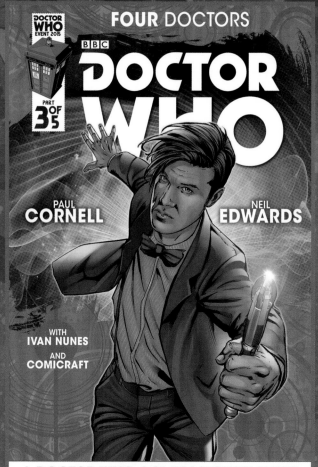

FOUR DOCTORS

DOCTOR WHO EVENT 2015
BBC

PART 3 OF 5

DOCTOR WHO

PAUL **CORNELL**

NEIL **EDWARDS**

WITH
IVAN NUNES
AND
COMICRAFT

A **DOCTOR WHO** COMICS **WEEKLY** EVENT

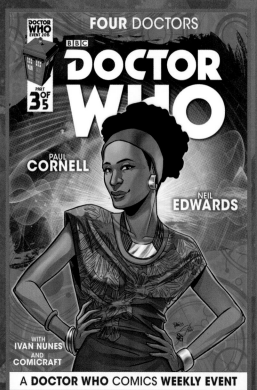

FOUR DOCTORS

DOCTOR WHO EVENT 2015

BBC

PART 3 OF 5

DOCTOR WHO

PAUL **CORNELL**

NEIL **EDWARDS**

WITH
IVAN NUNES
AND
COMICRAFT

A **DOCTOR WHO** COMICS **WEEKLY** EVENT

FOUR DOCTORS

DOCTOR WHO EVENT 2015

BBC

PART 3 OF 5

DOCTOR WHO

PAUL **CORNELL**

NEIL **EDWARDS**

WITH
IVAN NUNES
AND
COMICRAFT

A **DOCTOR WHO** COMICS **WEEKLY** EVENT

COMPANION Cover by Elena Casagrande,
Eleonora Carlini & Claudia SG Iannicello

SUBSCRIPTION Cover by
AJ & Rob Farmer

THIS TRENCH LOOKS LIKE SOMEONE *DUG* IT OUT.

YEAH. THIS ISN'T A BARE DESERT, IT'S A *MAZE*, A TRAP OF A DIFFERENT KIND --

-- SO EVEN IF WE'VE SOME-HOW CAUSED 'THE END OF THE UNIVERSE', SOMEONE STILL *WANTS* SOMETHING FROM US --

-- EVEN IF IT'S JUST TO KILL US.

DOCTOR --

-- I'M ALICE.

OH, I *LIKE* A FORMAL INTRODUCTION. PLEASED TO MEET YOU, ALICE.

DOCTOR!

YES! HELLO! RUNNING NOW! TRY TO KEEP UP! THOSE PLASMA BLASTS ARE COMING FROM OUTSIDE THIS REALITY, SO THEY'RE A LITTLE HARD TO ANTICIPATE!

BUT THE OTHERS--!

THEY'LL BE FINE. THEY BOTH HAVE ONE OF *YOU LOT* TO LOOK AFTER THEM.

LEGS ELEVEN'S GOT THE ONE WITHOUT ANY STRAIGHT LINES, YOU KNOW, THE SCHOOL-TEACHER ONE, SO THAT'LL PLEASE HIM.

HOW CAN YOU *SEE* PEOPLE LIKE--?!

YOU'RE USED TO A SKINNY, LOW CARB, FREE RANGE DOCTOR --

"-- I'M A BIT MORE *WHOLEMEAL*."

EVERY PATH LEADS TO A DEAD END --

-- EXCEPT ONE --

-- SO WE'RE BEING --

-- DRIVEN SOMEWHERE. YOU SAID HELLO EARLIER LIKE YOU ALREADY KNEW ME. *THIS* ME.

AH --

-- NO. I MEAN, YOU MUSTN'T KNOW --

IT'S A BIT LATE FOR THAT, CLARA, IF THAT IS YOUR REAL NAME.

OBVIOUSLY SOMETHING HUGE HAPPENS IN MY FUTURE. IT'S *BRILLIANT* THERE'S GOING TO BE ANOTHER ME.

THAT GINOR, WEIGHT SHOUL

AND IF THIS NEW ME WITH SOMEON NICE AS YO WELL --

-- HE *MUST* BE A VERY COOL SORT OF ME.

ALL SO... *COMPLICATED.* TELL YOU WHAT --

-- I THINK I PREFER TH RUNNING.

AL LIFE YOU 'THE UNIVERSE 'CHING IT OFF EN SWITCHING BACK ON AGAIN.

AGAIN, CAN'T SEE IT HAPPENING TO *ME*.

BUT HERE I... *GAVE IN*?

THIS DOESN'T LOOK SO BAD.

IT DOESN'T. BUT OUTSIDE, ALL OF HISTORY IS HAPPENING AT ONCE. I CAN *FEEL* IT. THE UNIVERSE IS DYING. AND I'M *LETTING* IT.

SO IF WE'RE TRAPPED IN *THIS* TIMELINE, THE PROPHECY CLARA FOUND WILL BE FULFILLED. GAME OVER.

WE'RE SWITCHING BETWEEN POSSIBLE FUTURES. IT'S NOT EVEN A PARADOX.

BUT DOESN'T THIS TIMELINE CONTRADICT THE LAST ONE? IF THE PREVIOUS YOU DIED --

PLEASE, NOBODY SAY 'TIMEY' ANYTHING.

WAIT A MOMENT, I CAN FEEL...

AH YES, HERE WE GO AGAIN. WHICH IS BOTH A RELIEF AND --

OH. OH, YOU... YOU CAME BACK.

I... DON'T KNOW WHAT I DID TO YOU. WHAT I WILL ONE DAY DO. BUT I'M SORRY.

YOU MUST KNOW WHO WE ALL ARE. DO YOU REMEMBER THIS?

WE'RE SOLID AGAIN. I PREFER SOLID.

I STIL HAVE A COMIC PHEW

I DON'T... REMEMBER...

SOMETHING ABOUT... NEEDING A LIFT? CLARA, MY CLARA, I WILL TAKE YOU ANYWHERE YOU WANT TO --

HOLD ON A SECOND --

-- I KNOW YOU, PAL. BETTER THAN I WANT TO. AND I DON'T TRUST YOU AN INCH.

OR, TO TRANSLATE --

-- YES, THANK YOU, WE WOULD VERY MUCH APPRECIATE A LIFT.

WE ALL HAVE SO MANY ASPECTS TO OURSELVES, I SUPPOSE.

THE DOCTORS GET TO SEE THEIRS FROM A DISTANCE.

THIS DISTRUST OF HIMSELF, THIS POTENTIAL TO BECOME SOMETHING TERRIBLE, TO *SETTLE* FOR SOMETHING *NOT RIGHT* --

-- I'VE SEEN THAT IN *MY* DOCTOR TOO.

I DON'T THINK GABBY KNEW THAT ABOUT HERS.

THAT ONE IS TRYING TO HIDE SO MUCH. HE'S RUNNING FROM HIMSELF. IT'S LIKE THERE'S A SHADOW OVER ALL OF THEM...

THIS '*TIME WAR*' THEY TALK ABOUT.

EXCEPT HIM.

HE'S DIFFERENT.

HE'S EITHER TURNED HIS BACK ON GRIEF AND SELF-DOUBT --

-- OR IT'S CONSUMED HIM *COMPLETELY*.

WE'RE OFF, CLARA! SOON YOU'LL SEE --

WE'VE MATERIALIZED INSIDE A VERY SMALL POCKET UNIVERSE, LESS THAN A HUNDRED MILES ACROSS.

SOMEONE MUST HAVE BUILT IT RIGHT NEXT TO THE CONTINUITY BOMB'S TIMELINE.

IT WAS THE ONLY WAY OUT I COULD FIND.

THE COORDINATES ARE ALL OVER THE PLACE...

YEAH, TO FIND A WAY INTO REGULAR SPACETIME, WE'RE GOING TO HAVE TO GO OUT THERE AND TAKE SOME DIMENSIONAL COMPASS READINGS.

GO OUT THERE?!

NO! I HAVEN'T LEFT THE TARDIS IN YEARS! IT MIGHT BE DANGEROUS!

WHY DID I HAVE TO GET THE COWARDLY TIMELINE?

PLEASE, LISTEN --

-- YOU'VE ALREADY BEEN BRAVE. WE NEED TO DO THIS TO GET HOME.

AND I THINK YOU COULD DO WITH THIS TOO.

AND HEY, IF WE'RE TALKING ABOUT SECURITY, HOW MANY DOCTORS DO YOU NEED?

IF... IF YOU SAY SO --

"-- I SUPPOSE IT MIGHT BE ALL RIGHT."

I DON'T RECOGNISE THIS STYLE OF ARCHITECTURE AT ALL.

AND WE'VE SEEN A *LOT* OF ARCHITECTURE.

THAT'S A TRANSPARENT FORCEFIELD, HOLDING BACK...

OH. NICE. A SEA OF ACID.

THAT PHRASE *SOUNDS*...

FAMILIAR. BUT IT *ISN'T*.

IS THIS WHAT DEJA VU IS LIKE? I'VE ALWAYS WANTED TO HAVE DEJA VU.

YOU'RE NOT MISSIN' MUCH.

HEY DOCTO

-- WELCOMING COMMITTEE.

DOCTOR WHO

'THE MEETING'

BY PAUL CORNELL & RACHAEL SMITH

COMPANION Cover by Elena Casagrande,
Eleonora Carlini & Claudia SG Iannicello

SUBSCRIPTION Cover by
AJ & Rob Farmer

"THEY HEARD THE MESSAGE OF THE TIME LORDS, THROUGH THE CRACK BETWEEN REALITIES.

"THEY REALISED THIS MEANT THE TIME LORDS MIGHT *RETURN*.

"AND *IF* THEY RETURNED, THEY MIGHT REVERSE ALL THE CHANGES OF THE TIME WAR.

"THEY MIGHT FORCE THE VOORD TO *LOSE* THEIR NEW POWER.

"SO A PLAN WAS DECIDED UPON. THE VOORD CONSTRUCTED A CITY IN WHICH TO SURVIVE --

"-- A CITY THAT CONTAINED *ALL* THEIR PEOPLE.

"THEY SURROUNDED IT WITH A FORCEFIELD THAT COULD LAST FOREVER."

"THEY TOOK A WEAPON FROM A DOWNED DALEK SAUCER --

"-- AND CONVERTED IT INTO AN ENGINE --

"-- AN ENGINE TO TAKE THE ENTIRE VOORD RACE OUT OF REALITY AND INTO THEIR OWN POCKET DIMENSION, WHERE YOU ARE RIGHT NOW --

"-- SO THE TIME LORDS, IF THEY RETURNED, WOULD *NEVER* FIND THEM.

"THEY VANISHED EVEN MORE THOROUGHLY THAN THE TIME LORDS HAD.

"THE VOORD MADE THE UNIVERSE *FORGET* THEY HAD EVER EXISTED."

"THEY FELT MY PAIN. THEY UNDERSTOOD IT. THEY COULD HELP.

"AFTER YEARS AMONG THEM, THEY OFFERED ME LEADERSHIP OF THE GROUP MIND.

AFTER CLARA LEFT ME, I SEARCHED FOR GALLIFREY. HOPELESSLY. I STARTED TO THINK THEY WERE *HIDING* FROM ME.

IN THE END I *DESPAIRED*. I LEFT THE UNIVERSE ENTIRELY --

-- AND HEARD THE VOORD CALLING TO ME.

"I STARTED TO FILL IN STRANGE *GAPS* IN MY MEMORY. I REMEMBERED THE CONTINUITY BOMB, REMEMBERED THAT MY HISTORY HAD ONCE BEEN *DIFFERENT*. THAT I WAS NOT *MEANT* TO HAVE FOUND THIS HAPPINESS WITH THE VOORD.

"I GRADUALLY REALIZED THAT I WAS TO BE *RESPONSIBLE* FOR WHAT HAD BEEN DONE TO ME.

"THAT NOW, FULL OF JOY IN MY NEW SITUATION, I HAD TO *MAKE* IT HAPPEN.

"THE VOORD COULD REACH BACK INTO THE MAIN UNIVERSE, TO *ANYWHERE* IN TIME OR SPACE.

"I USED THAT ABILITY TO PUT IN PLACE A 'MUSEUM', ITS COLLECTION TAKEN FROM MY OWN MEMORIES --"

"-- AND WITHIN IT, THE IMAGE I REMEMBERED, THE IMAGE THAT LED TO ALL THIS --

"-- THE IMAGE THAT WAS A TRAP OF MY OWN MAKING!"

TIMIEST, WIMIEST --

-- EVER.

SO, DO YOU ALSO REMEMBER ME STOPPING YOUR PLAN? AFTER KICKING YOU UP THE BACKSIDE?

THERE ARE STILL GAPS IN MY MEMORY. EVERYTHING AFTER I PUT ON THE HELMET JUST NOW... I DON'T REMEMBER YOUR SIDE OF THAT.

ONLY AFTER I FOUND THE VOORD DID I *REGAIN* THE MEMORIES OF WHAT HAPPENED AFTER THE CONTINUITY BOMB WENT OFF.

THESE GAPS *MUST* BE DELIBERATE. THIS *ALL* MUST BE PART OF *MY* PLAN.

HE'S TOUCHED US. SO NO BLINOVITCH. USE THAT... KEEP HIM TALKING.

WHY US THREE? IS IT JUST BECAUSE YOU REMEMBERED US FROM THE PICTURE?

I BELIEVE MY MEMORY OF THAT PICTURE WOULD BE OF WHATEVER IMAGE I LATER DECIDED ON.

ERM... POSSIBLY?!

I ONCE *SOUGHT* THE TIME LORDS. MY NEW PEOPLE NEED THEM TO STAY *LOST*.

YOU ARE THE THREE DOCTORS WHO MIGHT HAVE LOOKED FOR GALLIFREY, MIGHT HAVE *FOUND* IT, MIGHT HAVE CHANGED TIME.

BUT WHAT ABOUT, YOU KNOW, *BIG NOSE*? THE ONE BEFORE ME?

THERE WAS... A *PROBLEM* INVOLVING HIM.

AND I CAN'T LET *ANYTHING* GET IN THE WAY OF MY CHOSEN DESTINY.

YOU SEE, ONCE THIS IS DONE, *I'M* GOING TO BRING THE JOY OF THE VOORD COLLECTIVE MIND TO *EVERYONE.*

I AM GOING TO LEAD THE VOORD TO INVADE EVERY STRATEGIC POINT IN THE UNIVERSE, AT EVERY PERFECT MOMENT.

THEN *WE'LL* BE THE NEW TIME LORDS. BUT WE'LL TAKE *RESPONSIBILITY* FOR OUR DOMAIN. PEACE AND SAFETY *EVERYWHERE. EVERYONE* PART OF THE SAME *SPECIES.*

OH, WILL YOU *PLEASE SHUT UP?!* I GOT A GLIMPSE OF WORST *POSSIBLE* AND *DECIDED* TO *BECOME* HIM!

FORGIVE ME IF I DON'T SIGN UP TO YOUR MANIFESTO!

BUT YOU *WILL!* MY CENTURIES OF PAIN WERE *NECESSARY* FOR ME TO FIND MY *JOY* AND THE UNIVERSE TO FIND ITS *DESTINY* --

-- SO YOU FOUR WILL HAVE YOUR MEMORIES OF THIS WHOLE EXPERIENCE WIPED AND WILL BE PLACED BACK IN YOUR TIMELINES.

WHICH WOULD, RATHER HORRIBLY --

-- SQUARE WITH US NOT REMEMBERING ALL THIS, YES.

WHILE *YOU* WILL BE PLACED BACK IN YOUR TIMELINE WITH YOUR MEMORIES *INTACT...* UNTIL THE MOMENT THE BOMB WENT OFF.

YOU'LL ASSUME IT WAS FAULTY, THAT THE OTHER DOCTORS WENT BACK TO THEIR OWN TIMES --

YOU SUCCESSFULLY USED THE GLITCH TO ESCAPE THE CONTINUITY BOMB, JUST AS I REMEMBERED --

-- BUT YOU *WON'T* ESCAPE THE MENTAL COMMANDS I'M GOING TO IMPLANT IN *YOU.*

INCLUDING THE *COMPULSION* TO NOT *FORGIVE* CLARA'S BETRAYAL. TO THROW HER OUT.

I WILL MAKE SURE *YOU* BECOME *ME.*

I WILL MAKE SURE YOU ONLY SLOWLY *REMEMBER* THAT DESTINY.

FOR ALL THAT SUFFERING TO COME ...

I'M TRULY *SORRY.*

NEXT STOP: A DEVICE WE CALL *'THE CONSCIENCE'.*

THAT'S WHERE YOUR *MEMORIES* WILL BE ALTERED.

"-- TOGETHER!"

THE VOORD -- MUST MOVE --

THE CALL!

I ANSWER, LEADER!

PHEW! I THANK YOU --

"-- FOR YOUR HELP WITH THAT LITTLE DISTRACTION!"

HE'S FINE! HE KNEW WHAT HE WAS DOING, AS MUCH AS WE EVER DO, AH, YES, TOOK ME A FEW MINUTES TO EXAMINE THE TECH --

-- BUT NOW, WHILE THIS CHAP IS BUSY JOINING IN WITH THE GROUP MIND...

THERE WE GO!

WHEN I SAY --

SHE'S TRYING TO SOUND CONFIDENT, BUT... THIS IS MORE LOST THAN I'VE EVER FELT.

I DIDN'T GET THE DOCTOR'S SONIC, I GOT HIS COMICS!

IT FEELS LIKE A ENDING'S COMIN

THE ENDING OF A HORROR MOVIE.

WHAT CAN WE DO? WE'RE IN THEIR *UNIVERSE!* THIS HAS ALL *ALREADY* HAPPENED!

WHAT WOULD THE *DOCTOR* DO?

OKAY, SO... SO WHAT'S THE PLAN?

WE... WE NEED TO FIND THAT TARDIS --

-- THEN --

TRY TO RESCUE THE DOCTORS. OKAY.

IT FEELS LIKE WE'RE CLUTCHI AT STRAWS --

THAT'S WHAT *HAVING* YOUR *MEMORY* *ALTERED* FEELS LIKE --

-- AND IN A MOMENT --

-- YOU'LL FIND YOURSELVES --

I'VE *WRITTEN* THE STORY OF MY OWN *CREATION*

ALL THAT'S LEFT, JUST ONE TINY, THING.

ALL LEADING TO *ME!*

-- BACK IN THE UNIVERSE, FIXED IN YOUR *DESTINIES!*

"-- WE JUST HAVE TO FIND ALICE AND GABBY --

"-- AND EXTINGUISH, WITH THEM, *EVERY* OTHER POSSIBILITY."

IT'S NOT LIKE IT'S SOMETHING THEY CAPTURED --

-- IT'S THE LEADER'S *OWN* ARDIS, SO IT'LL BE SOMEWHERE --

-- OFFICIAL.

OKAY, SO THEY HAVE A GROUP MIND, SO NOBODY IS GOING TO STEAL IT, BUT STILL --

-- THAT LOOKS *VERY* LIKE A TRAP.

I HOPE I CAN BE AS BRAVE AS YOU, ALICE OBIEFUNE.

OKAY, THEN --

-- WE HAVE NO WAY TO SNEAK UP ON THAT. AND I DON'T EVEN KNOW IF MY KEY WILL FIT.

-- IF YOU FIND THEM AND I DON'T --

-- NO, *LISTEN* --

-- TELL HIM, TELL *MY* DOCTOR --

AND *IF* WE GET IN WE'LL HAVE TO PLEAD WITH... HOWEVER THE TARDIS IS NOW... TO FIND THE DOCTORS, SO, GIVEN ALL THAT, I'M GOING OUT THERE *FIRST*, OKAY? AND LISTEN --

-- THANKS. THANKS FOR SHOWING ME.

I WILL. AND IF --

-- THE SAME, OKAY? THE *SAME.*

OKAY, THEN...

FOUR DOCTORS

DOCTOR WHO EVENT 2015

BBC

PART 5 OF 5

DOCTOR WHO

PAUL **CORNELL**

NEIL **EDWARDS**

WITH **IVAN NUNES**

AND **COMICRAFT**

A **DOCTOR WHO** COMICS **WEEKLY** EVENT

FOUR DOCTORS

DOCTOR WHO EVENT 2015

BBC

PART 5 OF 5

DOCTOR WHO

PAUL **CORNELL**

NEIL **EDWARDS**

WITH **IVAN NUNES**

AND **COMICRAFT**

A **DOCTOR WHO** COMICS **WEEKLY** EVENT

FOUR DOCTORS

DOCTOR WHO EVENT 2015

BBC

PART 5 OF 5

DOCTOR WHO

PAUL **CORNELL**

NEIL **EDWARDS**

WITH **IVAN NUNES**

AND **COMICRAFT**

A **DOCTOR WHO** COMICS **WEEKLY** EVENT

COMPANION Cover by Elena Casagrande,
Eleonora Carlini & Claudia SG Iannicello

SUBSCRIPTION Cover by
AJ & Rob Farmer

SO... LET ME GET THIS STRAIGHT --

-- ALL YOU'VE JUST DESCRIBED --

-- WHICH, APPARENTLY, WAS YOUR FAULT --

HEY, I SAID *DON'T* LET THEM GO TO MARINUS --

-- BUT YEAH --

-- AT THE END OF ALL *THAT* --

-- YOU AVOIDED CERTAIN DEATH --

-- BY OPENING A PARCEL OF FRENCH COMICS?

YES, BECAUSE OF WHAT WAS *REALLY* INSIDE THAT PARCEL --

"-- SOMETHING THAT TERRIFIED ME --"

"-- A TINY WEEPING ANGEL."

NO! NO!

AHHHHHHHHH!

"TURNS OU[T] THEY CAN GROW."

IT MUST HAVE BEEN CHOSEN *DELIBERATELY,* AN ANGEL THAT SENT SOMEONE JUST THE RIGHT DISTANCE BACK DOWN THEIR OWN TIMELINE.

IT SENT ME *HERE.*

THAT'S... REALLY ME.

I BELIEVE HER.

AND I DON'T WANT TO DIE.

AND THIS IS ALL BECAUSE I GOT SUCKERED BY THAT PHOTO. OKAY, GABBY --

-- WE'LL PLAY IT LIKE YOU WANT US TO.

LIKE *I* WANTED TO IN THE FIRST PLACE.

WE FORGET THE PHOTO. NO MORE MARINUS.

THANK YOU! THANK --!

SHE'S GONE. WHY HAS SHE GONE?

OH, WAIT A SEC...

-- AND YOU'VE GOT THE "PACKAGE OF COMICS"?

YES, BUT --

IT'S OKAY. NOW WE WON'T NEED IT.

OH DEAR.

HEY, YOU TWO KEEP IT TOGETHER.

YEAH, NO POKING --

-- THEN WE WON'T HAVE TO GO THROUGH ALL THAT STUFF WITH THE REAPERS.

I'M SORRY I LED YOU INTO A TRAP. I'M SORRY I'M GOING TO... TO BETRAY YOU, SOMEHOW, BUT THE IMPORTANT THING IS --

-- IF WE CAN JUST AVOID GOING TO MARINUS, THEN NONE OF IT HAPPENS. THEN WE'VE WON ALREADY.

OH? YOU RECKON?

SHOW ME THE PICTURE.

I DON'T WANT YOU LOT--

SHOW ME!

[T]EMPTING.

BUT AVOIDABLE. FOR AGES.

WHAT, THOUGH, IS THE MOST IMPORTANT THING ABOUT THIS PICTURE?

OH WHY DON'T YOU TELL ME?

IT'S STILL HERE.

ONE CONTINUITY BOMB DETONATION AND GLITCH THROUGH THE THRONEROOM OF THE TIME LORD VICTORIOUS LATER...

SO WE MUSTN'T CHOOSE THE THIRD TIMELINE, AND I DON'T WANT TO CHOOSE THAT FIRST ONE --

WELL, OF COURSE WE SHOULD ALWAYS HAVE CHOSEN THIS ONE!

THIS IS EVERYTHING IN THE UNIVERSE THAT EVER EXISTED.

D'YOU THINK THAT MIGHT INCLUDE ANYTHING USEFUL? WHAT'RE THE ODDS?

OF COURSE! BUT WE'LL NEED --

-- TAXI FOR MR.GRUMPY!

VVOORRRP VVOORRRP

YOU TWO, CHOOSE T TIMELINE BY MAK US SOLID WITH "HIGH FIVE" O SOMETHING.

OR YOU COULD JUST, YOU KNOW --

"-- PUNCH EACH OTHER."

WE DON'T HAVE 'LONG' BEFORE THIS UNIVERSE COLLAPSES. FROM THIS GIANT TOOLBOX OF EVERYTHING, WE NEED TO FIND...

THERE IT IS. HANDY.

THIS IS IT, ANOTHER DALEK MONSTROSITY --

-- THE WEAPON THE VOORD ALTERED TO TAKE THEMSELVES OUT OF TIME AND SPACE.

AND WHAT *THEY* CAN DO--

-- AS LONG AS *YOU* STAY OVER THERE --

-- IF WE ALL JUST CONCENTRATE ON OUR OWN BIT --

AND WE ARE ON OUR WAY, OUT OF THIS UNIVERSE, HEADING BACK TO VOORD CITY--!

TAKE THIS ONE TO THE ENVIRONMENTAL UNIT, AND THIS ONE TO THE DIMENSIONAL CONTROL ROOM.

LEAVE THEM ALONE THERE. I WILL RETURN TO DO... *THINGS* TO THEM. *TERRIBLE* THINGS. THAT I CAN ONLY DO IN THOSE ROOMS.

BUT -- LEADER--!

YOU HAVE LOST YOUR CONNECTION TO THE GROUP MIND!

UNTIL ANOTHER HAS BEEN BIRTHED, THE MINE!

AH. YES --

-- PERHAPS I SHOULD HAVE MENTIONED. I THOUGHT THIS MIGHT HAPPEN.

THE REST OF YOU SHOULD PROBABLY --

-- RUN!

"-- BUT YOU'RE *NOT STRONGER* --"

"-- THAN ALL OF US --"

"-- *WORKING TOGETHER!*"

AH, RIGHT, *GROUP MIND.* I FEEL A BIT LIKE I'VE BEEN THROUGH A TEA-STRAINER, BUT I'M ON IT NOW. WORKING IN THE OUTSIDE WORLD AND IN HERE AT THE SAME TIME, TAKES A BIT OF DOING. *STILL!*

NOT ONLY DON'T YOU GET *CONTROL* OF THE VOORD, BUT *ZAP,* YOU'RE ALSO TRAPPED IN HERE.

IN THE OUTSIDE WORLD, HE'S JUST SWITCHED OFF YOUR CITY'S FORCEFIELD. YOU'VE GOT ABOUT AN *HOUR* BEFORE THE ACID EATS THROUGH THE OUTER WALL.

AND AS WE SPEAK, I'M FINISHING THE LINKS BETWEEN A REPROGRAMMED DALEK WEAPON AND THIS CITY'S *DIMENSIONAL CONTROLS...*

THAT'S THE *ONLY* OFFER WE HAVE FOR YOU.

THE ONLY WAY YOU CAN BE AT *PEACE.*

IF YOU TRULY *CARE* FOR YOUR PEOPLE --

-- TAKE THE SPECIFIC CONTROL I'M HANDING BACK TO YOU NOW, USE THE WEAPON TO *REGRESS* THE VOORD BACK DOWN THEIR TIMELINE --

-- OR IT'S *FRYING TONIGHT!*

RIS, 1923.

"I JUST THINK IT MIGHT BE NICE TO GO BACK TO THAT CAFE AND FINALLY HAVE A CREPE TOGETHER, BEFORE --"

AH, MAYBE NOT.

YOU KNOW --

"-- I RECKON I KNOW THE REAL REASON WHY *HE* WASN'T INVOLVED IN ALL THIS --"

"YES.

"THE VOORD COULDN'T FIND EVEN A *SINGLE* TIMELINE, IN ALL THOSE BILLIONS --

-- WHERE *HE* WAS ANYTHING OTHER THAN... FANTASTIC.

SO YOU'RE ALL GOING TO *FORGET*?

YES. MOST OF IT. A TIME LORD DEFENCE MECHANISM.

BUT YOU LOT WON'T.

YOU'RE GOING TO *REMEMBER*. AND THAT'S *BRILLIANT*.

OH?

WE'RE GOING TO LET THEM?

YEAH, WE ARE --

NOW WAIT

-- BECAUSE I STILL WORRY ABOUT HOW YOU CAME ABOUT --

-- BUT UNDERNEATH IT ALL, YOU'RE STILL *US*.

BYE BYE, EVERYBODY!

BYE CLARA! LOOK AFTER HIM!

YOU WERE AWESOME!

VWOORRRP

VWOORR

OH. IT'S STARTED. IT FEELS ALL... WARM AND FUZZY.

I KNOW I *LIKED* YOUR OTHER SELVES, BUT THE DETAILS OF WHAT HAPPENED AND... WHY... THEY'RE KIND OF... FADING.

I'VE NEVER FOUND IT A PLEASANT EXPERIENCE.

HEY, WHILE YOU STILL CAN, TELL ME --

-- WOULD YOU STILL WANT TO *BE* ANY OF THOSE GUYS?

WOULD *YOU* LIKE TO BE A TEENAGER AGAIN?

SOMETIMES.

I'M... DIFFERENT TO THEM.

THEY BOTH LIVED LIKE THEY HAD LIMITED TIME LEFT.

LIKE HUMANS, YOU MEAN?

YES, LIKE HUMANS --

-- IN THE *BEST* POSSIBLE WAY.

BUT YOU AND I, CLARA, WE CAN'T LIVE THE PAST.

WE MUST GO FORWARD --

-- TO THE *FUTURE!*

NOT THE END... EVER

DOCTOR SHOPS FOR ANGELS
L CORNELL & MARC ELLERBY

THE WEEPING ANGEL ...EUM OF THE YEAR FIFTY ...ILLION. HUNDREDS OF ...HOUSANDS OF THEM, ALL CONTINUALLY LOOKED AT.

NOW, WHERE'S THE ONE I ORDERED? WE HAVE TO GET THIS DONE BEFORE I *FORGET*.

HERE WE GO. EXACTLY THE RIGHT LENGTH OF TIMELINE SHUNT.

AND THEY'LL JUST LET YOU *TAKE* IT?

WELL, I DID *PROVIDE* MOST OF THEIR COLLECTION.

WE HAVE TO ARRIVE BEFORE PAST-ME DOES.

A VIEWING DEVICE IN THE PACKAGE WILL KEEP THE ANGEL DOCILE.

I DON'T THINK WE *HAVE* KNITTING FOR GIRLS.

SWITCH

AND I *FINALLY* GOT MY COMICS.

AH, PARIS. HAVE WE JUST GOT HERE? THERE'S THIS CAFÉ I KNOW...

AND ALSO, ALICE, REMIND ME TO PICK UP MY COMICS.

TIME!

FOLLOW YOUR FAVORITE INCARNATIONS ACROSS THESE FANTASTIC COLLECTIONS!

COMPLETE YOUR COLLECTION!

DOCTOR WHO: THE TENTH DOCTOR
VOL. 1: REVOLUTIONS OF TERROR

DOCTOR WHO: THE TENTH DOCTOR
VOL. 2:THE WEEPING ANGELS
OF MONS

DOCTOR WHO: THE TENTH DOCTOR
VOL. 3:THE FOUNTAINS
OF FOREVER

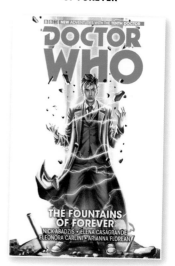

ISBN: 9781782761747
SALE NOW - $19.99 / $22.95 CAN / £10.99
(UK EDITION ISBN: 9781782763840)

ISBN: 9781782761754
ON SALE NOW - $19.99 / $25.99 CAN / £10.99
(UK EDITION ISBN: 9781782766575)

ISBN: 9781782763024
ON SALE NOW - $19.99 / $25.99 CAN / £10.99
(UK EDITION ISBN: 9781782767404)

COMING SOON!

DOCTOR WHO: THE NINTH DOCTOR
VOL. 1: WEAPONS OF PAST DESTRUCTION

DOCTOR WHO: THE EIGHTH DOCTOR
VOL. 1: A MATTER OF LIFE AND DEATH

ISBN: 9781782763369
COMING SOON - $19.99 / $25.99 CAN / £10.99
(UK EDITION ISBN: 9781782761056)

ISBN: 9781782767534
COMING SOON - $19.99 / $25.99 CAN / £10.99
(UK EDITION ISBN: 9781785851063)

AVAILABLE FROM ALL GOOD COMIC STORES,
BOOK STORES, AND DIGITAL PROVIDERS!

DOCTOR WHO

FOUR DOCTORS

BIOGRAPHIES

Paul Cornell is a writer of science fiction and fantasy in prose, comics and TV, one of only two people to be Hugo Award-nominated for all three media. He has written *Doctor Who* for the BBC ('Father's Day', 'Human Nature', 'Family of Blood'), *Action Comics* for DC, and *Wolverine* and *Captain Britain* for Marvel. He has won the BSFA Award for his short fiction, an Eagle Award for his comics, and shares in a Writer's Guild Award for his television writing. His urban fantasy novel series, from Tor, begins with *The Severed Streets*. He lives in Buckinghamshire with his wife and son.

Neil Edwards is a British comics artist whose skillful pencils have enlivened *Fantastic Four*, *Spider-Man*, *Justice League United*, *Legion of Superheroes*, *Dark Avengers*, *Iron Man*, and many more, including the forthcoming *Assassin's Creed: Trial by Fire*, also from Titan Comics.

Ivan Nunes is a Brazilian colorist whose past works have included Marvel's *New Avengers* and *Thor*, *Game of Thrones* and *The Bionic Man*.

Marc Ellerby is a British freelance illustrator and comics artist. As well as *Doctor Who*, he currently contributes comic strips to *Rick and Morty* and *Regular Show*.

Rachael Smith's first graphic novel, *House Party*, debuted to critical acclaim in 2014. Her second, *The Rabbit*, has just been released by Avery Hill Publishing. Rachael is also the creator of *Flimsy the Kitten* and *One Good Thing*. She is currently working on her new webcomic, *Bess*, at besscomic.tumblr.com.

Neil Slorance is an illustrator, painter and comics artist, and one half of the team behind the award-winning *Dungeon Fun* comic, now available in its first collection.

Colin Bell is a writer, letterer and publisher, who writes the regular *Twelfth Doctor* back-ups. As well as being the other half of the *Dungeon Fun* team, he also publishes comics under the DoGooder Comics label.